M000309187

The
WORST-CASE SCENARIO
POCKET GUIDE
SAN FRANCISCO

By David Borgenicht &
Ben H. Winters

Illustrations by Brenda Brown

CHRONICLE BOOKS
SAN FRANCISCO

Copyright © 2009 by Quirk Productions, Inc.

All rights reserved. No part of this book may be
reproduced in any form without written permission
from the publisher.

Worst-Case Scenario® and The Worst-Case Scenario
Survival Handbook™ are trademarks of Quirk
Productions, Inc.

Library of Congress Cataloging in Publication Data
available.

ISBN: 978-0-8118-7049-8

Manufactured in China
Designed by Jenny Kraemer
Illustrations by Brenda Brown
Visit www.worstcasescenarios.com

10 9 8 7 6 5 4 3 2 1

Chronicle Books LLC
680 Second Street
San Francisco, CA 94107
www.chroniclebooks.com

WARNING: You really should have been more careful. Now you're
facing one of the worst-case scenarios presented in this book—at least
you have the book with you, to refer to. But you must use your good
judgment and common sense and consult a professionally trained
expert to deal with these dangerous situations. The authors, publisher,
and experts disclaim any liability from any injury that may result
from the use, proper or improper, from the information contained
in this book. Nothing herein should be construed or interpreted to
infringe on the rights of other persons or to violate criminal statutes.
We urge you to be respectful and safe.

CONTENTS

INTRODUCTION

If you're going to San Francisco, be sure to wear some flowers in your hair . . . and for God's sake, watch your back. Sure, this is the city that gave the world the Summer of Love and delicious, harmless Rice-A-Roni, but when you get right down to it, Frisco is packed with dangers—starting with the scorn heaped upon you by the locals if you call it "Frisco."

But take heart. Whether you're trying to stop a runaway cable car, ride out an earthquake while stuck in an elevator, or disentangle yourself from a yoga pose gone wrong, this little book is going to be a big help. *The Worst-Case Scenario Pocket Guide: San Francisco* delivers crucial advice on important subjects such as how to stay warm in the summer, escape a sea lion attack at Fisherman's Wharf, and park on a hill—assuming you can find a space.

San Francisco is rightfully known for its liberal openness and proud peaceful heritage, the birthplace of the United Nations and the Grateful Dead. But it was also the birthplace of the novelist Jack London, a bleak realist whose stories are full of people freezing to death in the bitter cold. Now there was a guy who understood worst-case scenarios. And as London once said, "Life is not a matter of holding good cards, but sometimes playing a poor hand well."

We couldn't have put it better ourselves. Have fun—and good luck!

—The Authors

When you get tired of
walking around San Francisco,
you can always lean against it.
—Unknown

Chapter 1
Getting Around

AN UPHILL BATTLE

HOW TO STOP A RUNAWAY CABLE CAR

1 Run slightly ahead of the car.
Run alongside and just ahead of the right front side of the car. Even if the driver is incapacitated, a cable car attached to its cable will not be traveling more than 9.5 miles per hour.

2 Leap into the gripman's position.
Grab the vertical bar on the front right side of the car and use it to hoist yourself up and into the cable car.

3 Grab the grip lever at the front of the car.
The grip lever is a long metal pole emerging at an angle from the base of the cable car at the front of the vehicle.

Grab the vertical bar on the front right side of the car and hoist yourself into the cable car.

4 Pull backwards on the grip lever.
This will cause the cable car's grip to "let go" of the cable.

5 Operate the foot brake.
Press down on the foot brake located immediately behind the grip lever, causing the metal brake shoes to press against the wheels, slowing, and then stopping the cable car.

6 Pull the emergency slot brake.
Grasp the red grip to the left of the main grip lever and pull back as hard as possible, sending the emergency slot brake slamming down into the slot and bringing the cable car to a sudden halt. Hang tightly onto to the lever after you pull it to keep from being thrown off your feet.

7 Evacuate the cable car.

Be Aware

- A cable car weighs approximately 15,000 pounds, and has a passenger capacity of 60 to 70 people; a fully loaded car could weigh upwards of 30,000 pounds.
- Operating a cable car's grip lever is extremely difficult; only 30 percent of applicants to be cable car operators successfully get the job.
- Pulling the emergency slot brake is very rarely done; it is both very difficult to pull, and extremely difficult to get out once pulled. It pushes the brake down so far into the slot that it must often be removed with a torch.

HOW TO DRIVE IN THE FOG

1 Turn on your lights.
Do not turn on your high beams as the lights will reflect off the fog and create a glare.

2 Apply the brakes.
Decrease your speed to one half the posted speed limit. Avoid tapping repeatedly on the brakes as it may spook the drivers behind you.

3 Open the window.
Turn off the radio and ask other people in the car to be silent. Listen carefully for the sound of approaching cars.

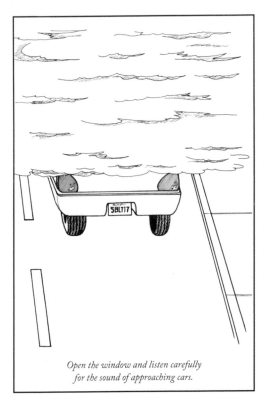

*Open the window and listen carefully
for the sound of approaching cars.*

4 Guide yourself by visible objects.
Watch as your lights illuminate lampposts, mailboxes, and lane markings, and use them to stay in your lane.

5 Increase your following distance.
When you see brake lights ahead, employ the "six-second rule": the moment the lights ahead pass a fixed object such as a lamppost, count slowly from one to six; if you pass the object before six seconds are up, decrease your speed.

6 Pull completely off the road.
If the fog continues to thicken, remove yourself from the road and turn on your emergency lights so other cars are aware of your presence.

Be Aware

• The rule of thumb for driving in the fog is to exercise the same caution as if you were driving at night, in a heavy rain: cut your speed in half, drive defensively, and pull off the road if conditions become extreme.

- The western parts of the city, such as the Sunset and West Portal, are foggier than the eastern and southern parts, as fog generally rolls in from the ocean and dissipates as it moves further inland.
- San Francisco can experience heavy fog in the summer, fall, and winter.

INSTANT SOLUTION

SURVIVE BEING CAR-DOORED

Throw your weight backward at the moment of impact.
Stand up on the pedals and apply the rear brakes only.
Turn your body to hit the door with your side
to disperse the impact.

HOW TO ESCAPE FROM A TRAIN STUCK IN THE TRANSBAY TUBE

1 Alert the authorities to the emergency using the intercom system.

Move to the front of the car and find the Attendant Call box. Press the button and then release it. When the attendant answers, describe the nature of the emergency and your train number, which is written on the intercom.

2 If there is immediate danger in your car, move to the next car.

To move from car to car, pull on the small rectangular handle on one or both halves of the sliding doors that separate the cars.

Follow the walkway until you reach a door.

3 | Open the exterior doors to your car.
If a fire or other danger is spread over several cars and no emergency help is forthcoming, remove the panel covering the door release lever, located above the seats next to the door. Move the door release lever in the direction of the arrow. The doors to the car will open.

4 | Look for a walkway.
If there is a walkway running alongside the track where the door has opened, exit the car; if not, move to another car, release the doors, and look for a walkway.

5 | Exit the train.
Climb down off the train, avoiding the high-voltage paddles that stick out from beneath the train, and access the walkway. Do not exit the train unless you have no other options.

6 Follow the walkway until you reach a door. Cross-passageway doors are painted bright yellow and occur every 300 feet. Yellow arrows along the tunnel wall show which way to go and how far it is until the next door. If a train passes while you are on the walkway, get down on all fours and wait until the train has completely passed before continuing to walk.

7 Go through the passageway to the opposite track.

8 Climb up onto the platform to safety.

Be Aware

- Emergency telephones are located throughout BART tunnels, and are marked with a blue light.
- The Transbay Tube is 3.6 miles long, and runs 135 feet below the San Francisco Bay.

MOST DELAYED MUNI METRO LINES

Line	Frequency of Delay
J	29%
M	26%
F	24%
K	21%
N	17%
L	10%

HOW TO PARALLEL PARK UPHILL

1 Look for an open space.
Repeat step as necessary.

2 Pull even with the car parked ahead of the open space.
Apply the brakes and put on your right turn signal to let the cars behind you know that you intend to park.

3 Measure the distance between you and the adjacent car.
Roll down your curb-side window and stick your arm out to ensure you are no closer than one arm's length from the car in front of the open space.

4 Put the car in neutral.
When the back of your car's front door is lined up with the rear bumper of the

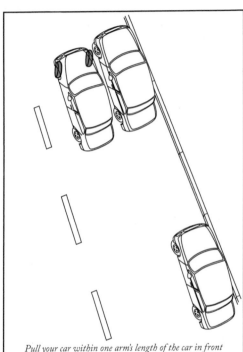

Pull your car within one arm's length of the car in front of the open space; turn your wheels to the right and roll down the hill in neutral toward the curb.

car ahead of the open space, stop the car.
Keep your foot on the brake to keep the
car from rolling down the hill.

5 Maneuver into the spot.
Turn the wheel one full turn to the right.
Ease off the brake to control your descent
and allow gravity to pull the car down-
hill and into the space. Adjust the wheel,
aiming your car for the right rear corner of
the open space. Stop when your rear wheel
touches the curb or rear bumper taps the
car behind you.

6 Pull forward and even out.
Turn the wheel one full turn to the left.
Put the car into drive, and ease from the
brake onto the gas. Pull forward and even
out the car's position in the space relative
to the curb. If the car is still uneven after
pulling forward, put the car in neutral and
repeat steps 5 and 6.

7 | Turn your tires towards the curb.
When you are fully in the spot, turn your steering wheel completely in the direction of the curb. If your space is on the left side of the street, point the wheel totally to the left.

8 | Put the car in park.

9 | Set your emergency brake.
In addition, if you have a manual transmission, leave the car in first or second gear; if you are driving an automatic, leave it in park.

Be Aware
If there is no curb along the hill where you are parked, place a block of wood under each of the front wheels to prevent the car from rolling away if the brakes should fail.

Steepest Hills and Their Grades

Filbert between Leavenworth & Hyde	32%
22nd Street between Church & Vicksburg	32%
Jones between Union & Filbert	29%
Duboce between Buena Vista & Alpine	28%
Jones between Green & Union	26%
Webster between Vallejo & Broadway	26%
Duboce between Divisadero & Alpine	25%
Duboce between Castro & Divisadero	25%
Jones between Pine & California	25%
Fillmore between Vallejo & Broadway	24%

INSTANT SOLUTION

WALK UP/DOWN HILL

Weave back and forth as you walk. When walking uphill, take short steps and maintain an upright posture. Avoid the urge to lean into the hill. When walking down, take long strides and lean forward slightly.

Chapter 2
The Bay

FOGGED IN

HOW TO RESCUE A WAYWARD WHALE

1 Disentangle the whale.

Maneuver your boat as close as possible to the fluke of the whale that has become disoriented and swum upriver rather than out into open ocean. Attach a curved blade, dull on the outside and sharp on the inside, securely to the end of a 10 to 15 foot pole, and cut away any fishing gear, nets, or traps that may be encumbering the whale. Move from the head of the whale to the tail.

2 Unbeach the whale.

If the whale has become partially beached on a shoal or mudflat, pilot a tugboat (or organize multiple tugboats) to travel in a figure-eight pattern just offshore of where the whale is stuck, creating enough of a wake to lift the whale off the shoal and back into open water.

3 Use *oikami* to drive the whale back to sea.
Drive the whale back towards the open ocean, and away from inlets and other upstream channels, by following the whale in a boat, or group of boats, filled with people banging on hollow steel pipes with hammers.

4 Guide the whale with whale feeding calls.
Lead the whale by broadcasting recorded whale feeding sounds from a boat heading toward open ocean.

5 Encourage the whale.
Arrange for people to gather on the coast and cheer or wave the whale.

6 Reunite the whale with its pod.
Trail the whale until it has relocated its migrating pod, especially if the whale is under 15 feet (and thus likely a calf).

Drive the whale back to the open ocean by banging on
hollow steel pipes suspended in the water.

Be Aware

- Humpback or other baleen whales normally follow a migration route from Mexico to Alaska, but often wander into the San Francisco Bay, where they can easily become entangled in fishing nets or crab traps.

- An adult humpback whale averages 40 to 50 feet in length and weighs about 80,000 pounds.

- A humpback whale stranded in freshwater can suffer skin damage, leading to infection, and risks starvation at a remove from its normal sources of food.

- Smaller animals, such as dolphins or porpoises, can be borne back into the water on stretchers.

SIGNS YOU'VE GONE TOO GREEN

Not Green	Green
Use incandescent light bulbs	Use compact florescent bulbs
Drink bottled water	Drink tap water
Baby wears disposable diapers	Baby wears cloth diapers
Dress in synthetic fabrics	Dress in organic cotton
Shop at supermarket	Shop at farmer's market
Cut down a tree	Protect a tree
Take long baths	Take short showers

Too Green

Limit activities to daylight hours

Drink only rainwater

Baby is free-range, au naturale

Wear outfits woven from your own hair

Dumpster dive

Live in a tree

Bathe at Ocean Beach

HOW TO ESCAPE A SEA LION ATTACK AT FISHERMAN'S WHARF

1 Back away slowly.
If the sea lion bares its teeth or moves rapidly towards you, back away from the animal.

2 Make a loud noise.
Stomp your feet and shout loudly to assert dominance or scare the advancing sea lion. Bang trash can lids, or use an accordion taken from a nearby street performer.

3 Distract the sea lion with food.
Toss available seafood items from the wharf toward the sea lion to distract it. Note that sea lions love fresh crab, but are less interested in sourdough bowls of clam chowder.

Use a street performer's instrument to scare the sea lion away.

39. *The Bay*

4 Move away from the water.

Sea lions can swim up to 25 miles per hour but they are much slower walking on their flippers across land. Run inland, away from the pier.

Be Aware

- Sea lions are not normally aggressive towards human beings, unless provoked. A charging sea lion is most likely a male who perceives a threat to its harem of mates. The sea lion may also be suffering brain damage from toxic algae.
- Sea lion bites often result in a condition called "seal finger," characterized by swelling and pain around the wound, sometimes leading to joint arthritis. Treat a sea lion bite with a course of antibiotics against bacterial infection.
- Sea lions can grow as large as six hundred pounds and eight feet long.

HOW TO CATCH A SPLASH HIT IN MCCOVEY COVE

1 Get into a prime position.
Pilot your kayak to the narrow inlet of San Francisco Bay, past the right field wall of AT&T Park. Arrive at least three hours before game time to beat other boaters to the prime home run–catching position, especially if a strong home run hitter is in either team's lineup.

2 Listen to the game.
Follow the game, listening to the play by play on a portable radio so you know when each batter is coming up and can be ready when a dinger is on its way out of the park.

Use a pole-length fishing net to retrieve the ball.

3 Maneuver into position.
Listen for the radio announcer to say things such as "it's going, going . . ." or "deep into right field . . . ." Aggressively paddle your kayak toward the right field wall. Keep your eye focused on the top of the wall and watch for where the ball sails over the wall.

4 Wield your net.
Stand in your kayak to extend your reach, and use a pole-length fishing net to catch the home run.

5 Paddle, position, and scoop.
If no one has successfully snared the ball, angle your kayak to block access to the ball from other kayakers and paddle to a position close enough to scoop the ball out of the water with your net. Stay in your kayak—you will be able to cover distance faster than if you left the boat and swam toward the ball.

6 | Distract the BARK dogs.

The stadium employs a team of Portuguese Water Dogs, known as the Baseball Aquatic Retrieval Korps, to retrieve splash hit home run balls. They leap from a motorboat called the *Good Ship Jollipup*, which cruises the bay during weekend games so the dogs can retrieve balls. Distract the dogs by throwing bones or tennis balls in their vicinity between them and the splash hit.

Be Aware

- It is considered bad form by other McCovey Cove dwellers and Giants staff to physically interfere with the BARK dogs.

- Kayaks have proven more maneuverable and effective in catching splash hits than motorboats or inflatable crafts or objects. Power boats are banned in the area.

- As of October 2008, 65 home runs have been knocked over the right field wall and landed in McCovey Cove; only 47 of those, however, were hit by Giants. Home runs hit by the opposing team are not considered true splash hits.

- During baseball season, temperatures in the cove are typically between 50 and 60 degrees Fahrenheit, but can dip as low as 30 degrees Fahrenheit with strong winds off the bay.

Signs Your Neighborhood is Becoming Gentrified

- Constant sound of cement mixers, espresso grinders.

- Restaurants replace ketchup bottles with candles, French fries with *frites*.

- Google shuttle bus picks up on the corner.

- Local homeless people wearing increasingly stylish cast-offs.

- Dive bar replaced by juice bar.

- Strollers get larger, more elaborate.

- You no longer live there.

HOW TO SURVIVE A WINDSURFING CAPSIZE UNDER THE GOLDEN GATE BRIDGE

1 Gather up your gear.
Collect your tow line, boom, mast, and sail, swimming swiftly before the tide can carry away your gear. Keep your board in sight at all times. If the water current is moving too swiftly for you to gather up the gear, let it go—the most important thing is not to lose the board itself.

2 Pile your gear on top of your board.
Wrap the tow line, boom, mast, and sail up into a big bundle. Lift the bundle up onto the board.

Pile your gear on top of your board and position yourself on top of the gear to hold it in place.

3 Heave yourself onto the board.

Securely grab onto one side of the board with both hands. Lift yourself above the water level with your arms, and then bring one leg at a time up onto the board. Position yourself on top of your bundle of gear so that you are holding it onto the board with your body.

4 Kick.

With the bundle of gear under your stomach, clutch either side of the board tightly with your hands and kick with your legs.

5 Navigate to shore.

Move due south toward San Francisco from the middle of the bay. Travel perpendicular to the shore, keeping the Golden Gate Bridge to your right at all times. Depending on how far out you were when you capsized, you will be between a mile and two miles from shore.

6 Land at Crissy Field.

Pull yourself and your gear out of the water at the edge of Crissy Field.

Be Aware

- Capsizing is often the result of equipment failure or lower extremity injury. If you have suffered the latter and cannot kick with your legs, paddle your board with your arms instead.

- Windsurfing is most challenging, and offers the highest risk, in heavy winds. You can gauge the amount of wind you will face under the bridge by the amount of fog you see rolling into the bay. The more fog, and the quicker it is moving, the stronger the wind.

HOW TO ESCAPE FROM ALCATRAZ

1 Tunnel a hole out of your cell.

Steal a utensil from the cafeteria and sharpen it by rubbing it against the cement floor. Remove the wall cover of your cell's air duct and, over a period of months, use the utensil to enlarge the shaft that connects your cell to the prison's ventilation system. Tunnel during daytime and evening hours when there is more general activity and ambient sound to mask the sound of digging. Replace the cover when you finish working.

2 Build a dummy of yourself.

Obtain magazines and newspapers from the library. After lights out each night, soak the magazines and newspapers in toilet water to create material for papier mâché. Sculpt a life-size bust of your head and upper torso. Decorate the head with flesh-colored paint from the arts closet and hair from the barbershop.

3 Arrange the dummy.
After lights out, place the dummy in your bunk, under the covers.

4 Crawl through your tunnel.
Remove the ventilation plate and enter the tunnel. Feel your way forward in the darkness of the shaft up the 30 feet to where the ventilation shaft ends at the roof.

5 Run east across the roof.
Run swiftly from the emergence point across the roof of the cellblock, avoiding the sweeping lights from the five guard towers that ring the building.

6 Climb down the cellblock.
Use the exterior piping to lower yourself down the 100 feet of the exterior of the

Run swiftly across the roof, avoiding the lights from the five guard towers.

53. *The Bay*

shower area, directly to the east of the main cellblock.

7 Sprint from the cellblock to the water.
Run past the recreation area to your left and the water tower to your right until you reach the eastern shore of the island, sloping downwards towards the water.

8 Scale the chain-link fence.

9 Dive into the San Francisco Bay.

10 Swim southeast.
Use a powerful crawl stroke and raise your hands as far out of the water as possible with each stroke to overcome the choppy water. The east end of the island does not have any undertow, but the tide can be extremely powerful, depending on the season and time of day.

11 | Head for safety.
Swim toward the Golden Gate Bridge, veering to the right towards the shore to avoid being pulled out sea.

12 | Arrive on shore.

Be Aware

- The water temperature in the bay averages 42 to 58 degrees Fahrenheit; at those temperatures, the average adult would contract hypothermia in about a half hour. Consider building a life raft and oars from materials such as raincoats, solvent, and brooms.

- When in operation, Alcatraz had a three-to-one guard-to-prisoner ratio, compared to the average federal prison rate of fifteen-to-one.

- Although there are sharks in San Francisco Bay, none are thought to be man-eating species.

CHAPTER 3
LIFE IN THE CITY

LET THEM EAT ARUGULA

HOW TO STAY WARM IN THE SUMMER

★ Dress in layers.
Regardless of the day's weather report, wear a tank top, T-shirt, button-down shirt, sweater, sweatshirt, and fall coat. Additionally, bring a winter coat with you. Adjust the number of layers you are wearing over the course of the day as necessary.

★ Bring an umbrella.
Carry an umbrella with you wherever you go, including the beach or on a hike. Also carry a towel to dry off after a sudden squall.

★ Carry hand-warmers.
Place them in the pockets of your shorts or in your shoes.

Dress in layers.

59. *Life in the City*

⭐ Maximize proximity to flame.
When at a barbeque or evening bonfire, sit as close as possible to the coals or fire pit.

⭐ Exercise vigorously.
Raise your internal body temperature by performing a quick set of 10 jumping jacks and 10 push-ups.

⭐ Modify the temperature of your household.
Place your air conditioner and heater side by side so that you can easily switch between one and the other when the weather becomes extremely cold or extremely hot.

Be Aware
The average temperature in San Francisco in June is 62 degrees Fahrenheit; in October it is 61 degrees Fahrenheit.

INSTANT SOLUTION

SURVIVE A SUPER BURRITO COMA

Stop eating. Save the rest of the super burrito for later by rewrapping in foil. Leave the taqueria and walk briskly in any direction. Drink water and belch.

HOW TO EAT SUSHI

1 Greet the host or hostess.

As you enter the restaurant, make eye contact with the person who welcomes you, and nod your head politely to any waiters or waitresses you see. It is not necessary to bow.

2 Sit at the sushi bar.

Greet the *itamae*, or "chef," in a measured, respectful tone.

3 Ask for the *omakase*.

Ordering the *omakase*, or "chef's choice," is a sign of respect, and the *itamae* will pre-pare a variety of sashimi (a bit of raw fish), *nigiri* (a bit of fish over rice), and *maki* (fish and rice rolled together in seaweed).

*Hold one chopstick between your thumb and middle finger
and the other between your thumb and forefinger.*

4 Order drinks, soup, and other nonsushi items from your waiter or waitress.
Never ask the *itamae* for anything other than sushi.

5 Do not ask the *itamae* to perform tricks.
Do not ask him to juggle knives or set a stack of onions on fire.

6 Eat with chopsticks.
When your sushi arrives, pick up your chopsticks. Hold one between your thumb and middle finger, the other between your thumb and forefinger. With a precise pincer motion, pick up one whole piece of sushi at a time. Eat each piece in one or two bites at most.

7 Pour two tablespoons of soy sauce in the shallow dish provided.
Dip your pieces of sushi sparingly in the soy sauce. If the *itamae* has preseasoned a piece of sushi, do not use soy sauce on it.

Between courses, ask the waiter or waitress (not the *itamae*) for a fresh bowl of soy sauce, especially if you have lost rice or pieces of fish in your soy sauce.

8 | Use wasabi sparingly.
Wasabi is a form of horseradish paste with an extremely strong taste that can overpower the delicate flavor of a piece of sushi. If the *itamae* has given you a piece of sushi with wasabi, do not add more.

9 | Freshen your palate.
Place a piece of sushi ginger, or *gari*, in your mouth between courses to freshen the palate. Do not eat the ginger along with a bite of the sushi.

10 | Finish everything on your plate.
It is disrespectful to leave uneaten sushi or sashimi on the plate, especially when seated at the sushi bar.

11 Place your chopsticks on the bar.
When you are finished eating, or while
waiting for more sushi, place your chopsticks on the bar in front of you, parallel
to the edge. Never insert and leave your
chopsticks in a bowl of rice, as this is
considered a bad omen.

Be Aware

- It is a sign of a superior sushi restaurant
  to offer finely grated fresh wasabi root
  rather than the green paste version.
- It is acceptable to eat sushi with your hands.

INSTANT SOLUTION

WALK IN HIGH HEELS

Step with your heel down first. Put one foot directly in front of the other and keep your toes pointed straight ahead. Shorten your stride and swing your arms to aid balance. Sway your hips.

HOW TO SURVIVE A SHOPPING SCRUM IN UNION SQUARE

1 Shop at the right time.
Plan your shopping for off-peak hours
and days. The crush of shopping crowds
increases later in the day and closer to the
weekend—shopping Monday morning will
be less intense than Friday evening. Note
that while sales on Black Friday (the day
following Thanksgiving) include "door-
busting" crowds at very early hours, these
crowds are generally self-contained and of
minimal threat to postdawn shoppers.

2 Research your items.
Although sale items are often only available in-store, you can still research your
selections online to narrow your shopping

Try on items using natural cover, such as large potted plants.

destinations from among the 2,000-plus retail outlets on the 2.6 acre plaza and its environs.

3 Remain focused.

Upon entering the store, go directly to the area and the item you are interested in. If visiting more than one department, start from the topmost floor and work down, and from departments furthest from the escalators to the closest to ease your movement between floors. Avoid slow and overcrowded elevators.

4 Grip your item(s) tightly.

Once you have selected something, hold the item tightly to your chest with both hands. If you are unsure which size will fit or color of the item you prefer, take one of each and move to a less-densely crowded area to sort through the items.

5 Avoid dressing room lines.

Try on items using natural cover, such as large potted plants or at the center of circular clothing racks, rather than wait in long dressing room lines.

6 Move immediately to the checkout.

Once you have selected your items, proceed directly to the closest register, holding your items close to your body, elbows out, head down.

7 Proceed to the next store.

Use your shopping bag as a wedge to help you make your way through the crowds to the next store.

Be Aware

Arrive at the store wearing comfortable shoes. Wear an appropriate under-layer of clothing for ease in trying items on in store aisles.

HOW TO TREAT YOGA MISHAPS

GET UNSTUCK FROM LOTUS POSITION

1 Take a calming breath.

Breathe in for a count of four, and then out for a count of four. Use your heartbeat to time the breaths.

2 Wedge your left hand beneath your right foot and your left thigh.

As you are removing the foot off the thigh, use your right hand to cradle the right knee.

3 Gently shift your right leg forward off the left thigh.

Fully extend your right leg and stretch your calf muscle. Rotate your ankle and wiggle your toes until you are sure your leg has not fallen asleep.

Chapter 3: Let Them Eat Arugula

Wedge your left hand beneath your right foot
and your left thigh and gently lift your leg.

4 Use your hands to lift and move the left leg.
Stretch out the left leg as you did the right.

5 Allow your muscles to relax before standing.

Muscle Cramp

1 Get out of the position.
Stop doing whatever pose has caused you to cramp and carefully reverse the movements that resulted in the cramp position.

2 Massage the cramped area.
Rub your hands in a gentle, circular motion over the cramp for one minute.

3 Stretch.
Extend the cramped area to its full length by standing up on tip toe (if suffering a leg cramp) or fully extending your arm (if suffering an arm cramp).

4 | Apply ice.
Wrap six chunks of ice in a headband and press against the cramping area. Rub the ice pack into the cramp for 10 to 15 minutes. Repeat steps 2 and 3.

5 | Drink water.
Drink eight ounces of water within a half hour of the onset of the cramp, and remain hydrated until the cramp subsides.

FORGOT YOUR MANTRA

1 | Remain calm.
If you cannot remember your mantra, let it go.

2 | Be here now.
Be present in mind and place. Survey the contents of the room and note three items or people.

3 Create a new mantra.
Combine the first syllable of the name of each item or person in the order you noticed them. This is your new mantra.

4 Recite the mantra.
Repeat your new mantra over and over until it loses its "meaning value" and transcends conscious thought.

5 After yoga class is over, write down your new mantra.

Be Aware

- Common yoga injuries involve the neck, hip flexors, and lower back. Rarer and more serious injuries include herniated discs and fractures, which can be caused by poses such as the plow and shoulder stand.
- Do not attempt more challenging versions, such as "power yoga," without the guidance of an experienced teacher.

Tech Talk

Instead of Saying	Say
Friends with	In-network
Thing	Gadget
Thing that does something	Widget
Commerce	E-commerce
New	2.0
Combination	Mashup
Conversation	Interface
Words	Text
Fired	Uninstalled

HOW TO SURVIVE AN EARTHQUAKE

INDOORS

1   Drop down on your hands and knees.

2   Crawl towards a sturdy piece of furniture.
Find a heavy desk or table with enough
room for your whole body to fit underneath.

3   Get under the piece of furniture.
If there is no such piece of furniture available, crawl to a section of wall that has no
high objects against it. Sit in a hunched
position with your back against the wall.

4   Cover your face and head with your
hands.

5 Remain still.
Close your eyes and stay in your safe spot
until the ground stops shaking. Remain
alert for aftershocks.

IN AN ELEVATOR

1 Drop down on your hands and knees on
the floor of the elevator car.
Assume a crouched position, covering
your head and face with your hands.

2 Stay in the elevator car.
Do not pry or bang on the doors. Most
California elevators are equipped with
shake-actuated switches that will automatically bring the car to the next level
and open the doors in the event of a quake.

3 Step off the elevator.
When the doors open automatically, look
down before you exit the car to make sure

Drop down on your hands and knees and assume a crouched position. Cover your head and face with your hands.

there is no gap between the door of the
elevator and the beginning of the floor.

4 Take shelter under a sturdy piece of
furniture.
Crawl under a heavy desk or table with
enough room for your whole body to fit
underneath. Cover your face and head
with your hands. Remain still and alert
for aftershocks.

On a Bridge

1 Stop the car.
Pull over either off the road or as far out
of the stream of traffic as possible. Turn
off the engine, set your emergency brake,
and turn on your hazard lights.

2 Remain in the car.
You will be more vulnerable to falling
debris if you are outside of the vehicle.

3 Prepare for possible submersion if the bridge collapses.
Roll all the windows of the car down completely. Remove glasses, shoes, jewelry, and heavy clothing. Switch on the car's interior lights.

4 Wait for the shaking to subside completely.
Stay inside the vehicle until the shaking has stopped.

5 Start your car and continue slowly.
Drive cautiously to the other side of the bridge, avoiding immobile cars, cracks in the roadway, and (once you are off the bridge) downed power lines. If the bridge has buckled in the course of the quake, exit your vehicle and walk rapidly away from the rupture to the other side of the bridge.

Be Aware
- Standing under a doorway is a common but mistaken reaction to an earthquake.

In most modern homes and apartment buildings, the doorway is no sturdier than the rest of the house.

- If you are in bed when an earthquake hits, stay in bed. Place a pillow over your head; you are far less likely to be injured by remaining in place.
- If you are not on an elevator when the quake begins, do not get on one. Use the stairs.
- According to the Working Group on California Earthquake Probabilities, California is more than 99 percent certain to suffer a quake of at least a 6.7 magnitude somewhere in the state in the next 30 years.

Bad Times to do Things

Activity	Timeframe
Shop on Kearny Street	Late February
Buy a costume, cross Howard Street	Mid-May
Tour the Mission District	Late May
Quit smoking marijuana	Second Sunday in June
Buy a feather boa, shop on Market Street	Late June
Swim at the beach	June through August
Get your bike fixed	Late summer
Buy chaps	Late September

Reason

Chinese New Year parade

Bay to Breakers

Carnaval

Haight-Ashbury Street Fair

Pride Parade

Summertime

Burning Man

Folsom Street Fair

HOW TO TREAT A SPRAINED ANKLE WHILE RUNNING BAY TO BREAKERS

1   Sit down.

Find a nearby spot to sit down on the curb, or atop another runner who has passed out from alcohol consumption.

2   Take off your giant chicken costume.

3   Ice the injury.

Take a handful of ice from someone's cooler or iced keg. Wrap the ice in a T-shirt and press firmly on the injured area for about twenty minutes or until the swelling goes down.

*Lie down horizontally on a bench and rest your
head on the torso of your costume.*

4 Compress the injured area.
Wrap the sprained ankle tightly with a makeshift bandage.

5 Lie down.
Assume a horizontal position on a bench, resting your head comfortably on the fuzzy torso section of your chicken costume. Elevate your ankles to about the level of the rest of your body. Remain in a horizontal position for 10 minutes and then try walking on the ankle to see if the pain is limited enough to allow you to continue.

6 Borrow or construct a crutch.
Find someone dressed as Little Bo Peep and borrow his staff. Continue along the race route.

7 Finish the race.
Do not push yourself to run too quickly; remember that Bay to Breakers is considered

the least competitive race in America, and possibly the world.

Be Aware

- During and postrace, continue to apply ice to the injury every half hour, for 20 minutes out of each hour, until swelling fully subsides.
- Do not combine any pain or antiswelling medication with alcoholic beverages.
- If you see someone dressed as a doctor or nurse, do not assume that they are actually a medical professional. Runners wearing low-cut nurse's gowns or "peek-a-boo" doctor scrubs should not be relied upon for medical treatment.
- The total race length is 7.46 miles.

INDEX

ACKNOWLEDGMENTS

David Borgenicht would like to thank Sarah O'Brien, Steve Mockus, Jenny Kraemer, Brenda Brown, and Ben Winters for making this book happen. You can be his cable car buddies anytime.

Ben H. Winters would like to first and foremost thank Lisa Alden, his personal SF guru. And to the many experts who guided him through the fog, including Tanya Houseman at the SFCVB, Judy Ann Lundblad of Ann's Driving School, Alcatraz expert Rich Weideman, Jim Oswald of the Marine Mammal Center, Ed Lyman, Fred Turner at the California Seismic Safety Commission, and windsurfer Fritz Muegenburg, whose pictures of the Bay at www.muegenburg.com you really should see.

ABOUT THE AUTHORS

David Borgenicht is the creator and coauthor of all the books in the *Worst-Case Scenario* series, and is president and publisher of Quirk Books (www.irreference.com). He has never left his heart in San Francisco, but he did once leave his laptop there. He lives in Philadelphia.

Ben H. Winters is a playwright, journalist, and humorist. He lives in Brooklyn, a.k.a. "Frisco on the Gowanus," where the burritos are good, but nothing like the real thing. You can pay him a visit at www.BenHWinters.com.

Brenda Brown is an illustrator and cartoonist whose work has been published in many books and publications, including the *Worst-Case Scenario* series, *Esquire*, *Reader's Digest*, *USA Weekend*, *21st Century Science & Technology*, the *Saturday Evening Post*, and the *National Enquirer*. Her Web site is www.webtoon.com.

MORE WORST-CASE SCENARIO PRODUCTS

VISIT THESE WEBSITES FOR MORE WORST-CASE SCENARIO PRODUCTS:

- ⊗ Board games
  www.universitygames.com
- ⊗ Gadgets
  www.protocoldesign.com
- ⊗ Mobile
  www.namcogames.com
- ⊗ Posters and puzzles
  www.aquariusimages.com/wcs.html

For updates, new scenarios, and more, visit:
www.worstcasescenarios.com

To order books visit:
www.chroniclebooks.com/worstcase

MORE WORST-CASE SCENARIOS

HANDBOOKS

- The Worst-Case Scenario Survival Handbook
- Travel
- Dating & Sex
- Golf
- Holidays
- Work
- College
- Weddings
- Parenting
- Extreme Edition
- Life

ALMANACS

- History
- Great Outdoors
- Politics

CALENDARS

- Daily Survival Calendar
- Daily Survival Calendar: Golf

POCKET GUIDES

- Dogs
- Breakups
- Retirement
- New York City
- Cats
- Meetings
- San Francisco
- Cars